ANYTHING
IS POSSIBLE
STUDY GUIDE

ANYTHING IS POSSIBLE

How Nine Miracles of Jesus
Reveal God's Love for You

STUDY GUIDE

JOBY MARTIN

with CHARLES MARTIN

FaithWords

New York   Nashville

FaithWords
Hachette Book Group
1290 Avenue of the Americas, New York, NY 10104
faithwords.com
twitter.com/faithwords

First Edition: March 2023

FaithWords is a division of Hachette Book Group, Inc. The FaithWords name and logo are trademarks of Hachette Book Group, Inc.

The publisher is not responsible for websites (or their content) that are not owned by the publisher.

The Hachette Speakers Bureau provides a wide range of authors for speaking events. To find out more, go to www.hachettespeakersbureau.com or call (866) 376-6591.

All Scripture quotations, unless otherwise indicated, are taken from the ESV® Bible (The Holy Bible, English Standard Version®), copyright © 2001 by Crossway, a publishing ministry of Good News Publishers. Used by permission. All rights reserved.

Library of Congress Cataloging-in-Publication Data has been applied for.

ISBNs: 9781546004622 (trade pbk.)

Printed in the United States of America

LSC-C

Printing 1, 2022

CONTENTS

Contents

A NOTE ON THE TEXT

Almost all direct Scripture quotes in this book come from the English Standard Version. In some cases I've simply paraphrased instead of quoting directly from a published translation; in these cases, the Scripture will be set in italics.

INTRODUCTION

I am delighted that you have chosen to use this study guide that was designed as a companion to my book, *Anything Is Possible*. The lessons, principles, and stories contained in this book walk you through nine miracles performed by Jesus—the miracle at the wedding of Cana, the story of the cripple at the pool of Bethesda, the feeding of the five thousand, the raising of Lazarus—as He teaches why we can believe God for a miracle (and how to deal with it when we don't get that miracle). This study is meant to help you look with fresh eyes at His signs and wonders and what they tell us, how they point us to the Father heart of God and His inconceivable love for us.

The thoughts and questions addressed in the following pages provide an insightful and spiritually rich examination of how each of the miracles of Christ teaches us something unique about how God wants to relate to us. Miracles are what happen when the unexplainable intersects the undeniable. When we face something we can't fix and run out of options, miracles are where the limited and finite ability of man ends and the infinite will of God begins. Where *what is impossible with man is possible with God.*

That God still does miracles today is based on the greatest miracle of all— the resurrection of Jesus. Because if the tomb is empty, *anything is possible.* Nothing is too hard for our God. As believers, we have access to the incredible power that raised Jesus from the dead, if only we tap into it.

No matter where you find yourself—whether you're a new believer or a seasoned servant of the faith, or maybe you don't know what you are—I'm so thankful you have decided to take this journey with me. Because we can't cover all the miracles of Jesus, I've chosen my favorite miracles to help you answer the following questions:

- Do you believe in miracles?
- Do you believe enough to obey?
- Do you believe Jesus will carry you?
- Do you believe Jesus can heal you?
- Do you believe even when doubts creep in?
- Do you believe Jesus can raise the dead to life?
- Do you believe Jesus is worthy of worship—no matter what?
- Do you believe Jesus is who He says He is?
- Do you believe God raised His Son to life?
- Do you want to know Christ and the power of His resurrection?

How you use this study guide will depend on the purpose you have in mind. You can work through it on your own for personal development or as a part of a small group study or discussion, say in a care group or book club setting. As you use this study to reflect on your life, I strongly encourage you to read each chapter in *Anything Is Possible* before you complete the exercises in the corresponding chapter in this study guide. Many of the questions are personal, and taking the time to read through the chapters in the book and think through how each question can affect your life will give the study immediate personal application. If you decide to use this study guide in a small group, go through each chapter on your own as preparation before each meeting. This will give your group study depth and make the sessions more productive for all.

Because of the personal nature of this study, if you use this guide in a group setting, remember that courtesy and mutual respect lay the foundation for a healthy group. A small group should be a safe place for all who participate. Some of what will be shared may be highly sensitive in nature, so respect the confidentiality of the person who is sharing. Don't let your conversations leave the small group. A small group is not a place to tell others what they should have done or said or thought, and it's not a place to force opinions on others. Commit yourselves to listening in love to one another, to praying for and supporting one another, to being sensitive to their perspectives, and to showing each participant the grace you would like to receive from others.

ANYTHING
IS POSSIBLE
STUDY GUIDE

Do You Believe in Miracles?

1. Jesus, the only begotten Son of God, willingly shed His blood on the cross to pay the penalty for our sins. What do the following Scriptures tell you about the blood?

> Leviticus 17:11
> Matthew 26:28
> John 19:34
> Luke 22:44
> Ephesians 2:13
> Romans 5:9
> 1 Peter 1:18–19
> 1 John 1:7

_____

_____

_____

2. Jesus climbed on the cross to drain the Father's cup of wrath and set us free from our slavery to sin. What do the following Scriptures tell you about what He accomplished there?

Romans 5:9
Isaiah 53:12
Isaiah 53:10
Hebrews 12:2
Colossians 1:13
Hebrews 12:24

_____

_____

_____

3. Jesus was arrested in a garden and buried in a garden. What is significant about what happened in those gardens? How does that relate to what happened in the very first garden?

_____

_____

_____

4. The most important question ever asked throughout history has been phrased many ways, but Pilate said it best: "What shall I do with Jesus who is called Christ?" (Matt. 27:22). How did C. S. Lewis answer this in *Mere Christianity*?

_____

_____

_____

5. If you answered that Jesus really is the Son of God who rose from the dead, what does that mean for you? How is the empty tomb the epicenter of everything in our lives? Is there anything that He cannot do?

_____

_____

_____

6. What are miracles? Write out Luke 18:27.

_____

_____

_____

7. You may be in a desperate place today where you need a miracle, where what you see is impossible. Why should you not fear and not give up? What difference does it make to believe, or *pisteuō*, in Jesus?

_____

_____

_____

8. What if the seemingly impossible thing you've been praying for is just on the other side of obedience? Read John 5:8 and Luke 6:10. Would you take Jesus at His word?

_____

_____

_____

9. Jesus, God made man, is alive. He's undefeated and undefeatable. And He is deeply in love with you. How does that change everything?

_____

_____

_____

10. In the kingdom of God, Jesus heals "every disease and every affliction among the people" (Matt. 4:23). Is Jesus still doing this? Can you find any expiration date in the Bible on the work of Jesus? Have you placed an expiration date on it?

_____

_____

_____

11. Read Daniel 3. What did it mean for Shadrach, Meshach, and Abednego to put their faith and trust in God? God allowed them to be thrown into the furnace, but what series of miracles resulted? How do you think you would have responded to the king's command to bow and worship the idol he had made?

_____

_____

_____

_____

12. Have you ever prayed that the Holy Spirit would help you believe despite what you can see? To what degree would you say you "walk by faith, not by sight" (2 Cor. 5:7)?

_____

_____

_____

_____

13. The empty tomb should encourage you to doubt your doubts and believe your beliefs. Explain what this means in practical terms. Give some personal examples.

_____

_____

_____

_____

14. Why did Jesus perform signs and wonders? What do they tell us?

_____

_____

_____

_____

15. Do you live in a world where the Son of God still does the miraculous and, because the tomb is empty, anything is possible, even when you can't see a possibility? Or do you live as though God just stuck us here and told us to endure the suck-fest all for His twisted amusement?

_____

_____

_____

_____

16. Paul told the Philippians, _I want to know Christ and the power of His resurrection_ (Phil. 3:10). So, what is that power? For us? Today? How is it a win-win-win all the way around?

_____

_____

_____

_____

17. Read Ephesians 1:15–23. When Jesus walked out of the tomb, He didn't just disappear. Where did He go? Where is He now? What amazingly powerful implications does this have for your life?

_____

_____

_____

_____

18. I invite you to join with me and pray the prayer at the end of the prologue. Take some time and write out what you sense God is speaking to you through this prologue.

_____

_____

_____

_____

CHAPTER 1

_____

Water into Wine—Do You Believe
Enough to Obey?

1. Read John 2:1–12. Even though Jesus hadn't performed a miracle yet, what did Mary know from the very first miracle that gave her the reason to say to Jesus, "They have no wine"? What did the angel tell her that is the basis for any miracle?

_____

_____

_____

_____

2. Despite Jesus' terse reply that His time had not come, what wise advice did Mary give the servants? Why is that the best advice we can receive in all of the Scriptures? Would you say that you live life based upon those words?

_____

_____

_____

_____

3. Describe the six stone water jars, what they were used for, and what the servants must have thought when they received Jesus' instructions on what to do.

_____

_____

_____

4. Changing the water to wine was the first of Jesus' signs or miracles. Why is this a big deal, and what is the stated purpose for this miracle, for any miracle?

_____

_____

_____

5. Just because you can't explain something, such as turning water into wine, or account for it scientifically or mathematically or medically or whatever, does that mean it didn't or can't happen? Given who Jesus is, how does His involvement change the equation?

_____

_____

_____

_____

6. When Jesus told the servants to take the jars, fill them, and take them to the host, which came first—the miracle or their obedience to His word? What does that say about any step of obedience God is asking you to take? Think of it in terms of a miracle you are praying for.

_____

_____

_____

_____

7. When was the last time you acted upon what Jesus told you to do even when it made no sense to you? Take your time and give this an honest review. Why does this matter?

_____

_____

_____

8. Jesus didn't just turn the water into wine so the wedding party could go on. It was a sign pointing to something. How does that something connect to the dirty water?

_____

_____

_____

_____

9. The Bible begins (Gen. 2) and ends with a wedding, and the first sign occurs at a wedding. Weddings matter to Jesus. Read Revelation 21:1–6 and 19:6–9. Those of us who have surrendered to the Lordship of Jesus Christ are headed to the most epic party in the history of parties. To His wedding. What did His bride cost Him? How does the wine of the Lord's supper depict that?

_____

_____

_____

_____

10. When Jesus spoke of the "cup of the New Covenant," how does that contrast to the Old Covenant? How does that underscore the fact that Jesus is the only way to God?

_____

_____

_____

11. _Gethsemane_ means "the place of crushing." How crushing was it for Jesus in Luke 22:41–44?

_____

_____

_____

12. How is the covenant between God and His church different from a contract, which is how most people define their relationship with God?

_____

_____

_____

13. By changing the water to wine at the wedding in Cana, what if Jesus wants to show throughout all human history a picture of what it looks like to be invited to the great wedding supper in Heaven (Rev. 21:1–6; 19:6–9) to which every single person, no matter what you believe, no matter what you've done, no matter how you grew up, is invited? If we are the dirty water, how are we changed to the best wine?

_____

_____

_____

14. You have been invited into a covenant relationship with God. Jesus' invitation to believe in Him and come and follow Him is the most important decision you will ever make. If you're ready to admit that you need a Savior and that you believe that Christ is that Savior, then right now, on behalf of Jesus, I would like to invite you to come. The Bible says, *Believe in your heart that Jesus Christ was raised from the dead and confess Him as Lord* (Rom. 10:9). Take some time and write out what's on your heart to Him.

_____

_____

_____

_____

15. Whether you've been a believer for five minutes or five decades, I also invite you to follow my instructions on taking Communion. It matters that you regularly take time to participate in His death and resurrection, as Jesus says, "in remembrance of Me." What does the breaking of the bread remind us of and bring us to?

_____

_____

_____

_____

16. When our Lord Jesus held up the cup of wine, what was He fulfilling and also cutting? How is this a mind-shattering paradigm shift? What does it point to?

_____

_____

_____

_____

17. Now take the bread, break it, and eat it as the body of Jesus broken for you. Take the cup and drink as the blood of Jesus shed for you. Bow your head, close your eyes, and let its meaning soak in. Write a prayer of thanks and praise that Jesus paid the price for the forgiveness of your sins.

_____

_____

_____

_____

CHAPTER 2

The Paralytic—Do You Believe Jesus Will Carry You?

1. Have you ever been desperate? Completely without hope? With no chance of it ever getting better? Describe one of those times. How did you respond? What was the result?

_____

_____

_____

2. Read Mark 2:1–12. How desperate was the man who was lowered through a roof to Jesus?

_____

_____

_____

_____

3. Given the signs and miracles and wonders, Jesus' ministry was in full effect. Why was He performing these? Was it to wow the crowds?

_____

_____

_____

4. What did the four friends of the paralytic have to be willing to do in order to get him before Jesus? Put yourself in the room beneath them as they tear off the thatched roof above. How pleased do you think you would have been?

_____

_____

_____

5. There will come a day when you cannot make it on your own. Where you find yourself paralyzed by fear or doubt or a financial situation or a health crisis or a relational situation. Today, do you have four friends who will carry you to Jesus? What are their names?

_____

_____

_____

_____

6. What is the difference between a buddy or a girlfriend, or a casual friend and a spiritually significant friend? Name at least four things a true spiritual friend will do for you that casual friends won't.

_____

_____

_____

_____

7. If you don't have friends like the paralytic's friends, how do you plan to get to Jesus when you're paralyzed? What are you doing to find such friends? Where will you find them?

_____

_____

_____

_____

8. Mark 2:5 says that "when Jesus saw their faith." What constitutes faith?

_____

_____

_____

9. Why was Jesus' first word to the paralytic, "Son"? How is this reflected in John 9:2–3? Bottom line, don't we often believe that same line of reasoning?

_____

_____

_____

10. How would addressing the paralytic as "son" have affected his identity?

_____

_____

_____

11. The religious elite got in an immediate uproar when Jesus said, "Son, your sins are forgiven." What was their reasoning on this, and why was Jesus essentially saying, "You're absolutely right"?

_____

_____

_____

_____

12. Was it easier for Jesus to say the man's sins were forgiven or to tell him to rise up and walk? What point was He making that would eventually get Him killed?

_____

_____

_____

_____

13. Why were the Jewish rabbis unable to logically dispute what Jesus said and did?

_____

_____

_____

14. What is the natural response when we see God for who He really is?

_____

_____

_____

15. The four friends each held ropes attached to the corners of the paralytic's mat. Corner Number One is sharing your faith. Do you personally share your faith? Do you tell the story of what Jesus has done in you and through you to people who need Jesus? If not, why not?

_____

_____

_____

_____

16. Read Acts 1:8. You are the "witness" who receives the power of the Holy Spirit to share your faith. The same Holy Spirit that resurrected Jesus from the grave lives in you and wants to lead, guide, and direct you to share your faith. List some of the ways that the Spirit has led you to share your faith.

_____

_____

_____

_____

17. In what way do you feel the most comfortable sharing your faith? In what ways would you like to improve?

_____

_____

_____

18. Read Matthew 28:18–20. In what ways do you see yourself being engaged in this Great Commission in the future?

_____

_____

_____

19. Corner Number Two of the mat is serving in your local church. Read Ephesians 4:11–12. Who has God given to serve the church, and what is their purpose?

_____

_____

_____

20. How have you been equipped for the work of ministry, and how are you contributing to the building of the church?

_____

_____

_____

_____

21. In Matthew 16:18, Jesus says, *On this rock I will build my* ecclesia. What is He saying? How has that unfortunately been changed by how we understand "church"?

_____

_____

_____

_____

22. Corner Number Three is bearing the stretcher—being willing to tear a hole in the roof, if that's what it takes to bring others in need to Jesus. Are you willing to make a mess and disrupt the comfortable who already have a seat in order to make room for one more?

_____

_____

_____

23. Are you willing to do whatever it takes to make room for everybody in the church, including those who don't look, dress, talk, or act like you?

_____

_____

_____

24. Did Jesus require that people believe in Him or look like Him in order to hang out with Him? How do you translate that to the church you're involved with? Can people walk into your church dirty or must they be cleaned up first?

_____

_____

_____

25. Read John 12:32. How is this statement the secret to church growth? How does your church do that? How do you do that?

_____

_____

_____

_____

26. Compared to a medical triage, describe what the church should hopefully look like. Who is Jehovah Raphah (Exod. 15:26), and what is the role of the saints regarding Him?

_____

_____

_____

27. Corner Number Four is for God to do what God does. Read Ezekiel 36:26. Why is this the crucial corner that makes the other corners have any value?

_____

_____

_____

28. Read John 15:13–16. In what remarkable way is Jesus different from all the religious leaders throughout history? Because the tomb is empty, is what Jesus did for the paralytic any less available to us?

_____

_____

_____

29. Are you in need right now? Are you paralyzed with fear? Are your finances wrecked beyond repair? Do you have a health problem? Are you living with a secret sin that you've held on to for years and shame is paralyzing you? Describe your need.

_____

_____

_____

30. Perhaps it's time to reach out to your four friends (or one friend), invite them to your home, and open up your need to them. Then bring all that to the feet of Jesus. What does Hebrews 4:16 tell us to do?

_____

_____

_____

31. When Jesus said "It is finished" from the cross (John 19:30), what happened to the curtain in the temple (Matt. 27:51)? Why is that so incredibly important?

_____

_____

_____

_____

32. Is one of your friends in need? Is the Lord nudging you to call two or three other friends and go to that person? Why don't you become the hands and feet of Jesus and bring that paralyzed person to the Father? When was the water turned to wine? When was the paralytic healed? Won't you be the friend to do that for your friend?

_____

_____

_____

_____

33. I invite you to join with me and pray the prayer at the end of this chapter. What are you believing that God is doing in you that only He can do? Take time to spend with Jesus, your Jehovah Raphah, and let Him bring you the healing and hope you need.

_____

_____

_____

_____

CHAPTER 3

Healing at the Pool of Bethesda—Do You Believe Jesus Can Heal You?

1. Is your body sick or damaged? Your heart broken? Even your memories? Jesus often asked this question, so let me ask you: Do you want to be completely healed? Write the name of the thing that you want to be healed.

_____

_____

_____

2. Read John 4:46–54. What does *an official* mean? What was the official asking Jesus to do? What was Jesus' response?

_____

_____

_____

_____

3. What did Jesus not say in response? Where was His focus?

_____

_____

_____

_____

4. This official has money, power, and prestige, but when his son is at the verge of death, what can't heal him? How desperate is this father?

_____

_____

_____

5. For a parent, there is no pain like kid pain. When something's wrong with your child, you begin to ask yourself, _Is this all about me? Are they suffering because of my sin or mistake or mess-up?_ Ever experience that? Describe it.

_____

_____

_____

6. Read Luke 15:11–32. How does the parable of the prodigal son show that kid pain sometimes has nothing to do with what the parent has done or not done?

_____

_____

_____

7. Have you ever had a son or a daughter, a mom or a dad, a spouse or a loved one, at the point of death and you're crying out to God, "Jesus, please come down before my child dies"? Describe it as well as what happened.

_____

_____

_____

8. How did Jesus answer the official? Why was He not bothered by the fact that the boy was not there physically?

_____

_____

_____

9. Based on Jesus' word alone, the official believed Him and went home. What didn't he ask Jesus?

_____

_____

_____

10. Do you see yourself responding as this official did? Do you believe that Jesus is able to heal you or your loved one?

_____

_____

_____

11. If you said no, you don't believe, then do you want to believe? Are you willing to be willing? What really good news is it that Jesus never measured someone's faith to see if it was sufficient? Is it the amount of faith you have that matters?

_____

_____

_____

12. Read Mark 9:23–24. What makes this perhaps the most honest prayer in all Scripture? Is an itty-bitty faith, when unbelief seems bigger than belief, a hindrance to Jesus?

_____

_____

_____

13. In John 4:50–51, how does the official demonstrate what faith is? How does that tie in with what the apostle Paul says in Philippians 4:6–7? How does that tie in when the doctor's report isn't good?

_____

_____

_____

14. The official's story didn't end there. It says that he believed "and all his household" (John 4:53). How does this tie in with Romans 8:28? How does God use the worst mess for His own message?

_____

_____

_____

15. This was "the second sign that Jesus did" (John 4:54). What sign was He demonstrating?

_____

_____

_____

_____

16. Read John 5:1–17. Comment about the multitude that was scattered around the pool of Bethesda like pickup sticks. What does that say about the people whom Jesus spent His time with? Whom did He come for?

_____

_____

_____

_____

17. Jesus' attention was drawn to a man lying by the pool who had been an _invalid_ for thirty-eight years. That was a life span in the first century, and that was how the culture would have seen him—as an "IN Valid" human being. How did Jesus see him? What value sticker does He put on every single human being on this planet? See 1 Corinthians 6:19–20.

_____

_____

_____

18. The problem of pain and suffering is a question we all wrestle with. Understanding the five categories of pain can help you deal with it and better know how to pray. The first category is understanding that we live in a fallen world. What has been the consequence of sin entering the world?

_____

_____

_____

19. The second category of pain is demonic attack. Read Ephesians 6:10–20. Are you aware of the spiritual battle that you are in? Whether it's an addiction, criticism or false accusations about you from others, or an oppression, what battles do you fight?

_____

_____

_____

_____

20. Read 2 Corinthians 10:3–6. Are you ready for this fight? Are you equipped with the divine power to destroy the strongholds of the enemy? Explain your answer.

_____

_____

_____

_____

21. The third category of pain is the effect of our own sin. Describe a painful part of your life that was or is self-inflicted.

_____
_____
_____

22. The fourth category is the pain we suffer when others sin against us. Describe a situation where your pain was the result of someone else's sin. How do you keep from having a victim mentality?

_____
_____
_____

23. The fifth category of pain is the suffering that comes from the hand of God to work His purpose in our lives. How is this seen in the following verses?

    2 Corinthians 12:7–10
    1 Samuel 16:14
    Psalm 105:17–19
    Job 1 and 2
    Isaiah 53:5
    Genesis 50:20

_____
_____
_____

24. When Jesus asked the invalid, "Do you want to be healed?" (John 5:6), what did He mean by "healed"?

_____
_____
_____
_____

25. In order to be healed, the "want to" comes before the "how to." Why is it that people in pain often really don't want to be healed?

_____

_____

_____

26. What is the invalid's response to Jesus' question? How does Jesus mercifully cut through this man's excuse and bring him to the real answer to his pain?

_____

_____

_____

27. What are some of the means that God uses to bring healing? What is the source?

_____

_____

_____

28. Why does Jesus tell the man to take up his gross and nasty mat and carry it wherever he went? What does it mean that only Jesus gets to tell you who you are?

_____

_____

_____

29. Jesus doesn't tell the man to ever lie back down on the mat. Liken that to the life of a believer.

_____

_____

_____

30. The Jewish religious leaders could not see past their Sabbath rules in order to see the miracle, to see the lavish love of God. Have you seen a similar problem among "church people"? Ever seen the problem in yourself? In what ways?

_____

_____

_____

31. Read Mark 7:1–13 and Isaiah 29:13. What warning was Jesus giving the self-righteous Jewish leaders that we need to heed as well? How deeply rooted are your traditions?

_____

_____

_____

32. When Jesus meets with the no-longer-crippled man, He tells him, "Sin no more, that nothing worse may happen to you" (John 5:14). What might He be indicating? What is worse than being on that mat for thirty-eight years?

_____

_____

_____

_____

33. Through the inspiration of the Holy Spirit, James says this to you: "Is anyone among you suffering?...Is anyone among you sick?" (James 5:13–14). How comprehensive is the word _sick_? What are you suffering from? Is there anything in your life that is broken, sick, or out of line from what God would desire and design for you? Describe it.

_____

_____

_____

_____

34. The Bible says, "Hope deferred makes the heart sick" (Prov. 13:12). Do you feel hopeless about something that's important in your life? What is it? Where is hope found?

_____

_____

_____

35. What can you take from the prayer of Shadrach, Meshach, and Abednego to help you in praying for healing?

_____

_____

_____

36. Read James 5:17–18. What qualifies you to pray?

_____

_____

_____

37. Read James 5:14–16. This is God's promise to you, and I want to close this chapter by praying for your healing. If you're by yourself, find some olive oil and put it on your own head as a symbol of the Spirit of God on you, then pray the prayer at the end of this chapter with me. If you know someone who believes the Word of God is true and walks in obedience, ask them to pray with you. If you're in a faith community, call your church and ask them to anoint you and lay hands on you. As you pray the prayer at the end of this chapter, let this be my prayer over you, and just let the Holy Spirit have His way. When you finish, give God the praise and stand fast in your healing. Write a declaration of what you have believed God for.

_____

_____

_____

CHAPTER 4

The Feeding of the Five Thousand—Do You Believe Even When Doubts Creep In?

1. I want to ask you to put yourself in Sgt. Ike Brown's place. Stare at that courtroom and his son's killer through Ike's eyes. What are the whispers screaming in your head? What happens when life just doesn't make sense? What do you do when your doubts are raging?

_____

_____

_____

2. Read John 6. When Jesus asked Philip about buying bread to feed the multitude, what does it mean that "He said this to test him"? Read Hebrews 12:5–11. Why does He test and discipline us? Whatever you're facing, what can you rest assured about the Father?

_____

_____

_____

_____

3. What did the little boy understand about what looks like an impossible situation that the disciples didn't? What powerful lesson was he showing?

_____

_____

_____

4. Are you trusting Jesus with what He's put in your hand? Or do you believe you can do a better job with it than Him? Are you white-knuckling or open-handed?

_____

_____

_____

5. The Bible says that Jesus took the bread, took the fish, gave thanks, and then handed the fish and the loaves to the disciples and said to them, *"You feed them."* Twenty thousand hungry people. Where does the miracle happen? Has God ever called you to do something that you think may make you look like an idiot?

_____

_____

_____

_____

6. What has God put in your hand that He wants you to give to others? What stewardship is He calling you to today?

_____

_____

_____

7. When the people saw the sign that had been done, their intention was to take Jesus by force and make him king. Why are we so prone to want Jesus to be on our team, to support our cause? Why does that never work?

_____

_____

_____

8. Seeing Jesus walking on the water on the raging Sea of Galilee in the dark, the disciples heard Jesus speak the most repeated command in the Bible: "Do not be afraid" (John 6:20). According to the apostle Paul in 2 Timothy 1:7, what is fear? What is the difference between fear and being frightened?

_____

_____

_____

9. When Jesus enters the boat, immediately the boat was at the land to which they were going. It had been one epic miracle event after another. But often the deepest valleys in the Bible come off the highest mountaintop experiences. Name three of these in the Scriptures and what happened.

_____

_____

_____

_____

10. Whether we are on a mountaintop or in a valley, does the location have any bearing on the presence of God with us?

_____

_____

_____

_____

11. At this point, with so much going on, thousands were rowing and walking from all over the region to follow Jesus. What does Jesus tell the crowd in John 6:26–27? What is He ultimately saying?

_____

_____

_____

12. What does the "abundant life" in Christ mean, and what does it not mean?

_____

_____

_____

13. Why do all religious people want to ask Jesus what they must do to perform the works of God?

_____

_____

_____

14. Why is this the wrong question, and what is the right question?

_____

_____

_____

15. What does Jesus say is the work of God we must do? What is the only thing that will satisfy us deep down?

_____

_____

_____

16. After experiencing two super-legit miracles, the crowd asks Jesus to show them another sign. What does that say about what is needed for true belief?

_____

_____

_____

17. The crowds had not lifted their eyes above their physical needs and saw only bread. When Jesus says, "I am the bread of life; whoever comes to me shall not hunger, and whoever believes in me shall never thirst" (John 6:35), why does His statement turn the discussion on its head and blow their minds?

_____

_____

_____

18. Read John 6:37–40. While this statement may raise some theological issues for you, what reassurance does Jesus' statement give you about God's power to keep you? Does God draw us or do we have to decide? How amazing is it that God is drawing you to Jesus?

_____

_____

_____

19. When the religious people grumble about who Jesus says He is versus what they understand about Him, what does He tell them that is very unpopular to say today?

_____

_____

_____

20. Jesus reiterates to the Jews that not only is He the bread of life, but that "truly, truly, I say to you, unless you eat the flesh of the Son of Man and drink his blood, you have no life in you" (John 6:53). How did the Jews interpret what He meant, and what must Jesus' disciples have been thinking?

_____

_____

_____

21. Jesus told those in the synagogue that to abide in Him they must *feed on My flesh and drink My blood* (John 6:54) without explaining His meaning. Is He required to give us explanations? How is this a reminder of how we are saved?

_____

_____

_____

22. While Jesus does not give an explanation, He gives a hint in John 6:62 that is the key to understanding this text. What is it, and how is this often His answer to what we don't understand?

_____

_____

_____

23. Many of Jesus' disciples turned away from Him at this point. Why doesn't He try to stop them? Why do you think they walked away?

_____

_____

_____

24. Jesus even asks the twelve disciples if they want to leave as well. Have you ever felt like walking away from Jesus because He said something hard (John 6:60) or He didn't do what you thought He should do? Perhaps it's an illness or depression or a betrayal or a financial problem or an addiction that won't go away. You've prayed and believed, but nothing has changed, and you don't understand. Describe a situation you've found yourself in that made you want to walk away and give up.

_____

_____

_____

_____

25. We all have our pain and our doubts. What does the enemy want you to believe? What does faith in Christ require you to believe?

_____

_____

_____

26. How is Simon Peter's answer to Jesus' question the answer of a true disciple?

_____

_____

_____

27. What happens when you base God's love for you on your circumstances? What must we base it upon, even if our circumstances are horrible and painful?

_____

_____

_____

28. Back to Sergeant Ike's story. As hard as it is to imagine, how did Ike live out an empty-tomb faith that crushed the darkness surrounding him as well as Takoya?

_____

_____

_____

29. Could you write the letter that Ike wrote? Why does Ike's response make no sense in the natural world, yet it is the gospel?

_____

_____

_____

30. I'm sure that as you've worked your way through this chapter, any doubts you have and any things in your past that make no sense have risen to the surface and whispered in your ear. So what are they? I want you to name what tempts you to doubt God's love for you and those you love, and makes you want to walk away from Jesus.

_____

_____

_____

_____

31. Now I want you to lay down your doubts and again participate in the Lord's supper. When Jesus said, *Unless you eat My flesh and drink My blood,* He was pointing at what we call "communion" and at what communion means to us. We are going to lay down our doubts and pick up the body and blood of Jesus in exchange. So I want you to follow the instructions that I've provided at the end of this chapter. Keep remembering what Jesus did on the cross in payment for our sins and keep receiving His forgiveness.

_____

_____

_____

_____

32. I invite you to join with me and Ike and pray the prayers at the end of this chapter. Then write your own prayer and commit what you have laid in God's hands and give thanks that God will work in all the painful, unexplainable things for your good.

_____

_____

_____

_____

CHAPTER 5

The Raising of Lazarus—Do You Believe Jesus Can Raise the Dead to Life?

1. Read John 10:7–18. As a backdrop for this chapter, describe what qualifies Jesus to be the Good Shepherd.

_____

_____

_____

_____

2. What was Jesus' relationship with Martha, Mary, and Lazarus?

_____

_____

_____

_____

3. That Jesus loved Lazarus and that Lazarus was sick were both true. What does that tell us about God's love for us?

_____

_____

_____

_____

4. When you are in pain as Martha and Mary were, is prayer for you a first response or a last resort? What does Hebrews 13:15 tell us about how we need to start out every day, whether we're on the mountaintop or in the valley?

_____

_____

_____

5. In the light of Hebrews 5:8, if God loves us, why would He allow us to walk through pain?

_____

_____

_____

6. No matter the reason for our suffering, how is Romans 8:28 true for every single one of us? What does this Scripture mean?

_____

_____

_____

7. When a painful situation hits, we tend to focus on our circumstances and say, "God, what are You doing?" What do we need to remember about His love for us as demonstrated in our current circumstances?

_____

_____

_____

8. When Jesus hears that Lazarus is sick, what do we expect He will do? How does His delayed response show that our belief and God's cooperation in our pain and suffering are not related?

_____

_____

_____

9. Have you ever cried out to God over and over and over, believing that He loves you, but He didn't answer your prayer right away . . . or He didn't show up at all. Describe your experience.

_____

_____

_____

10. Do you believe that whether or not God's timeline intersects with yours has no relation to His love for you? Explain your answer.

_____

_____

_____

11. Despite how bleak things looked for Lazarus, what does Jesus say is ultimately going to happen?

_____

_____

_____

_____

12. The disciples repeatedly did not understand what Jesus was telling them, yet they keep stating their ignorance. Have you ever tried to explain to God how the world works? What is a better use of your time?

_____

_____

_____

_____

13. How was Thomas one step ahead of the other disciples as to actual discipleship?

_____

_____

_____

14. Lazarus had been in the tomb four days by the time Jesus arrived. Why did He wait?

_____

_____

_____

15. Describe the difference between Martha's and Mary's personalities.

_____

_____

_____

16. Despite Lazarus being dead, Martha still believed that God would give Jesus whatever He asked for. She had a plan for Jesus. Name a time when you gave God your plan.

_____

_____

_____

17. Martha has correct doctrine, which matters because you can't love God rightly without right thoughts about God. So why is she still missing Jesus? How does Jesus redefine eternal life in a way that she hasn't understood?

_____

_____

_____

_____

18. Jesus looks at Martha and says, "I am the resurrection and the life," and then He asks her, "Do you believe this?" Why is this *the* rubber-meets-the-road question for Martha and for each of us?

_____

_____

_____

19. How does Martha's response indicate that she's starting to understand? What is she seeing?

_____

_____

_____

20. What does Hebrews 6:19 tell us about our faith?

_____

_____

_____

21. How is Mary's coming to Jesus different from Martha's, even though the words are the same? Describe a time when you've been in pain and could only ask, "God, what are You doing?"

_____

_____

_____

22. What does Jesus' response to Martha's and Mary's questioning Him tell you about your own questioning of God?

_____

_____

_____

_____

23. King David prayed, "My God, my God, why have you forsaken me?" Ever felt that way? Why does God want the real you, with all the intensity you can muster?

_____

_____

_____

24. "When Jesus saw [Mary] weeping, and the Jews who had come with her also weeping, he was deeply moved in his spirit and greatly troubled" (John 11:33). What is the difference in meaning between the *compassion* of Jesus and the Greek word used here, which is *embrimaomai*?

_____

_____

_____

25. Have you ever been so moved and yet so mad that you cried? What was it that brought Jesus to this great compassion and anger?

_____

_____

_____

26. "Jesus wept" (John 11:35). Sit with that thought and just let it soak in. What does that and Ecclesiastes 3 tell you about the role of emotions in your life?

_____

_____

_____

_____

27. Jesus sat with Mary, put His arm around her, and He just wept. Do you weep with those who weep, hurt with those who hurt, as Jesus did? Why is it a good idea to not worry about words and just shed some tears with them?

_____

_____

_____

28. Do you equate crying with weakness or strength? Is it hard for you to empathize and express your emotions?

_____

_____

_____

29. What does it mean that Jesus weeps and yet He knows that He is about to resurrect Lazarus?

_____

_____

_____

30. What is it that makes Jesus' command to "take away the stone" (John 11:39) the rubber-meets-the-road moment of faith? How does that reflect moving from the theoretical to real life?

_____

_____

_____

31. What stone do you need to roll away? Has God called you to do something you are not doing (which is called disobedience) because you are afraid it might be stinky? What is He calling you to do with Him so He can resurrect Lazarus?

_____

_____

_____

32. How is Lazarus' resurrection a picture of our salvation and a reflection of Ephesians 2:4–10?

_____

_____

_____

33. After Lazarus was called out of the grave, why was Jesus' first command to him to take off his grave clothes? What does that mean?

_____

_____

_____

34. One of the things the enemy is going to try to do to you is define you by your scars and by your past wounds, past sins, and defeats. What is yours? What good news does Isaiah 61:10 tell you that God has done?

_____

_____

_____

35. When Jesus has called you out of the grave, He is the only one who has a right to define who you are. What do you need to put away from the past to walk in a manner worthy of the gospel of Jesus Christ?

_____

_____

_____

36. What does Dr. Asher mean when he says he's "living the Lazarus moment"?

_____

_____

_____

_____

37. Do you believe Jesus can heal? Raise the dead to life? Today? Right now? In your life? Something in this chapter has touched a nerve with you that you know you need to bring to God. Maybe you need to bring your questions to Him, to be real and to let the tears flow. Maybe you've been called to come alive for the very first time and come out of the grave. Maybe you need to take off the old grave clothes. Whatever it is, my one request is that you pray with somebody you trust. If you don't have anybody, call our church and our people will pray with you. God has called each of us into a family of faith to help us take off our grave clothes and walk in the newness of life. So grab somebody's hand and pray with Dr. Asher and with me at the end of this chapter. Pour it all out at the feet of Jesus and let Him redefine who you are and make you new.

_____

_____

_____

_____

CHAPTER 6

Mary Anoints Jesus—Do You Believe Jesus Is Worthy of Worship—No Matter What?

1. In John 11:45, what effect did seeing Lazarus resurrected have on many of the Jews? How was the same true for Job after his trial (Job 42:2–5)?

_____

_____

_____

2. Not all who saw believed. How did some of the others react? Can you imagine their responses? How do you think it is even possible?

_____

_____

_____

_____

3. What was the response of the chief priests and the Pharisees when they heard Jesus had raised Lazarus from the dead? What was their only concern, and how is this the heart of every man-made religion?

_____

_____

_____

4. The religious leaders made and enforced the rules. Why were they so upset with Jesus?

_____

_____

_____

5. What was Caiaphas' counsel, and how was his statement theologically correct?

_____

_____

_____

6. How can God use someone who is ungodly, such as Caiaphas, to teach the truth? What is the bigger picture here?

_____

_____

_____

_____

7. The decision by the religious leaders to kill Jesus comes down to what? While that sounds bad, how do we struggle with the same thing?

_____

_____

_____

_____

8. Describe what it means to follow Jesus, to be one of His disciples.

_____

_____

_____

_____

9. We fear losing control of our life, yet Jesus requires us to deny ourself. What would it look like, right now, for you to deny yourself? What is He calling you to deny that you are hanging on to?

_____

_____

_____

10. Why did Jesus lay low at this point until the Passover? Read Exodus 12:1–32 and John 1:29. What had John the Baptist made perfectly clear about who Jesus was and what He would do for us?

_____

_____

_____

_____

11. Six days before the Passover, Jesus returned to Bethany, where Lazarus had been raised from the dead, where Jesus had said to roll away the stone. I asked you, "What stone is Jesus telling you to roll away by faith?" Was it doubt and unbelief? Did you roll it away, or did you refuse to take your hand off the reins of your life?

_____

_____

_____

_____

12. Read Mark 14:3. Why is it significant where the dinner for Jesus took place? What is this party about? How should a church, an ecclesia, be the same?

_____

_____

_____

_____

13. How do Martha, Lazarus, and Mary all respond differently to the presence of Jesus? In which of the three ways are you mostly wired? Why should all three be evident in the life of a believer?

_____

_____

_____

14. Describe how Mary worshiped Jesus so beautifully. What was she saying in doing so?

_____

_____

_____

15. The point of Mary's worship was her love for Jesus. How does our love for Jesus change everything? Read Psalm 42:1–4. Does your soul long for God like this?

_____

_____

_____

16. Take some time to contemplate Jesus' death on the cross and how He continuously lavishes His love upon you. Can you take it in? Does your love of Jesus Christ well up in you to the point that it overflows with tears that pour out onto His feet? Do you sing as a man or woman who was dead and is now alive?

_____

_____

_____

17. How does real worship change the atmosphere of a service as well as our heart?

_____
_____
_____

18. How does Judas react to Mary's worship? What is the danger in criticizing the way others worship? What is the danger of how we handle our finances as well?

_____
_____
_____

19. Describe some of the differences between being a consumer of Christianity and a worshiper of Jesus.

_____
_____
_____

20. In what ways have you struggled with making your church experience about meeting your needs and enjoying experiences rather than coming as a worshiper?

_____
_____
_____
_____

21. As you read the quotes from St. Augustine, Luther, Spurgeon, Owen, and Brother Lawrence, what resonates in your heart?

_____
_____
_____
_____

22. What did Mary understand about Jesus that Judas never did, despite being one of the twelve disciples? What warning should we take from this?

_____

_____

_____

23. Jesus said to Judas, "For the poor you always have with you, but you do not always have me" (John 12:8). Was Jesus not pro poor people? Read Matthew 25:31–46. What is His point here about the role of service and worship?

_____

_____

_____

24. What are the three things that the enemy wants to destroy?

_____

_____

_____

25. Read John 4:23–24. It's easy to get hung up on a style of worship. What is God looking for from you? Are you okay with singing "when heaven meets earth like a sloppy wet kiss"?

_____

_____

_____

_____

26. When Mary worships Jesus, she is modeling what our response should be for Him. The church is the bride of Christ, who is our groom and gave His life for us, and He's coming back to take us home. If the prodigal's father covered his son's face with kisses, isn't our Father God also inviting us into a passionate love? Will you let Him?

_____

_____

_____

27. What are you grateful to God for? Where are you on the continuum between gratitude and entitlement?

_____

_____

_____

28. This chapter is not telling you to jump up and be happy when you are devastated by loss and pain and suffering. But even when you hurt like hell in a world filled with the collateral damage from sin, what does Hebrews 13:15 instruct us to do?

_____

_____

_____

29. When we don't understand and our heart is broken, what assurance are we given in Hebrews 12:28? Why can we choose to just praise Him?

_____

_____

_____

30. What do King David, Job, and Paul and Silas show us about worship?

_____

_____

_____

31. I invite you to pray the prayer at the end of this chapter and to write a prayer of your own as well. You may be walking through the valley of the shadow of death and need to worship your way through this tough time. You may need to break your jar of nard and pour it out upon the feet of Jesus. Bring whatever God has been speaking to your heart about and lift your eyes to Jesus, the lover of your soul.

_____

_____

_____

_____

CHAPTER 7

The Bleeding Woman—Do You Believe
Jesus Is Who He Says He Is?

1. Have you ever been so desperate that either God shows up or you're toast? Desperate in the sense that you've tried everything, called every doctor, and spent every penny, and yet you can't fix your own problem? Describe it.

_____

_____

_____

2. Malachi, the last book in the Old Testament, is God's last word to His children before four hundred years of silence. It closes the Old Testament, but it does so with a promise of more to come. The promise of a sequel. What does Malachi 3:16 tell you about the remnant in Israel as well as God's care for them and for us?

_____

_____

_____

3. The Lord writes our name in the Book of Life, but why doesn't He write how He will reward us according to our righteous deeds? Rather than record all our sins and failures, what does He record?

_____

_____

_____

4. What does "imputed righteousness" mean?

_____

_____

_____

5. What remarkable statement does God make about us in Malachi 3:17? Do you believe that that is who you are? So how much does God treasure you?

_____

_____

_____

_____

6. How does Romans 8:31–32 express the statement, "And I will spare them as a man spares his son who serves him"?

_____

_____

_____

_____

7. How does Malachi 3:18 and the parable of the sheep and the goats in Matthew 25 speak of a separation and a day of judgment?

_____

_____

_____

8. What unpopular truth is stated in Malachi 4:1? What do you say to someone who says, "We're all going to heaven"?

_____

_____

_____

9. When Malachi continues, "And you shall tread down the wicked, for they will be ashes under the soles of your feet, on the day when I act" (Mal. 4:3), what is the Lord saying? What kingdom principle is involved (Matt. 6:10; Rom. 16:20)?

_____

_____

_____

10. How does Malachi 4:4 answer the question of how a New Testament believer relates to the Old Testament law?

_____

_____

_____

11. God says, "Remember the law of my servant Moses." What does the apostle Paul say about the role of the law in his life in Romans 7, then answers it in Romans 8:1?

_____

_____

_____

_____

12. What two people does Malachi promise are coming? How long do the Israelites wait for God to speak again? What does that say about God's timetable?

_____

_____

_____

_____

13. Read Luke 1:5–17, with a focus upon verses 16–17. Why should Zechariah have been ready for the coming Messiah? How was his son tied to Malachi's prophecy, and what was the significance of his name?

_____

_____

_____

14. How did John the Baptist prepare the way of the Lord, and what did he state about Jesus in John 1:29? Why was this mind-blowing?

_____

_____

_____

15. When Jesus was baptized, what did God the Father say about Him before He did any earthly ministry? How does God love us the same way?

_____

_____

_____

_____

16. What three things did Jesus primarily do during His earthly ministry?

_____

_____

_____

_____

17. How did the people react to Jesus the same back then as they do today?

_____

_____

_____

_____

18. Read Luke 8:40–55. Describe the desperation of Jairus, the father of the dying twelve-year-old girl. Have you ever felt that type of desperation? Describe it.

_____

_____

_____

19. Contrast Jairus with the woman who had had a discharge of blood for twelve years. What does this tell you about the people who make up the kingdom of God? Who matters, and who doesn't matter?

_____

_____

_____

20. This woman has been labeled as "the woman with the issue of blood." Why does the world label us by our issue? Does God refer to us by our issue rather than our miracle?

_____

_____

_____

21. How has the world labeled you? Who is the only one who has the right to tell you who you are? Who are you not?

_____

_____

_____

22. Describe the desperate situation of this woman. What did Jesus represent to her? How were her hopes fulfilled?

_____

_____

_____

23. Anyone in that society who had an issue of bleeding was considered unclean, yet when she touches the purity of Jesus, she is made clean. How is the same true with our issue of sin?

_____

_____

_____

24. Lots of people in the crowd were bumping up against Jesus, but what does He say made this woman's "touch" different? She was the only one in the crowd who was healed. What does that tell you is possible when you gather with others in the presence of Jesus?

_____

_____

_____

25. Why was this woman so afraid when it became clear that she was the one who touched Jesus? Read Leviticus 15:19–25. How serious was this?

_____

_____

_____

26. What do you need to understand if you ever have a pastor or church leader look at you and say, "What are you doing here?" No matter what your condition, will Jesus let you grab ahold of Him for healing?

_____

_____

_____

27. How does Jesus dispel this woman's fear? How does He define her? How does He define you?

_____

_____

_____

28. Jesus would have been wearing a Jewish prayer shawl that day. The "fringe of the garment" was a little tassel thing called a *knopf* in Hebrew. Read Malachi 4:1–2 again, which everyone in Israel knew was speaking of the coming Messiah. What is special about the word *knopf* here?

_____

_____

_____

29. Describe this woman's sense of anticipation as she elbows her way through the crowd. What has she heard about Him? Would she let her fear paralyze her faith?

_____

_____

_____

_____

30. When she reaches out to Jesus, what does she grab, and what does she discover?

_____

_____

_____

_____

31. Read Matthew 17:20. How much of your faith is required in order to see something change? What is it about your faith that changes things?

_____

_____

_____

32. This woman was instantly healed physically, but what else did she need Jesus to heal? How does He speak to that need? How does He speak the same to us?

_____

_____

_____

_____

33. The Son of righteousness, Jesus, has risen with healing in His wings. So do you need to be healed? If so, is your healing waiting on the other side of a small step of faith as hers was? Do you need to elbow your way to Jesus?

_____

_____

_____

_____

34. There are many areas of our life that require healing. This woman's need was physical. Others are spiritually dead and need to surrender themselves to Jesus as Lord. You may need Jesus to mend a broken relationship, a broken marriage, or a friendship. Your finances may be broken. You may need mental healing when you believe the labels the world has given you. You may need emotional healing for depression and anxiety. What need makes you want to reach out and touch Jesus? Describe it.

_____

_____

_____

_____

35. This woman fought through the crowd and I want you to do the same. Make it known right now and touch Jesus. Drive a spiritual stake in the ground. Tell someone who is a believer. Let them know that you need prayer and healing. Call someone. Text someone. Email someone. Email me (joby.martin@coe22 .com) and some folks from our church will pray with you. Who are you going to contact, and what exactly are you going to ask them to pray with you about?

_____

_____

_____

_____

36. Jesus says, "Whatever you ask in my name, this I will do, that the Father may be glorified in the Son. If you ask me anything in my name, I will do it" (John 14:13–14). As you're praying, I want you to pray as though everything depends on it, because it does. Ask it, and receive it. God Almighty says to you, "Son or daughter, your faith has healed you. I have a purpose and a plan and a peace for you." Now join me in the prayer at the end of this chapter and let me pray for us. Then write a declaration of what you have asked for and received.

_____

_____

_____

_____

CHAPTER 8

The Empty Tomb—Do You Believe God
Raised His Son to Life?

1. What is the greatest miracle of all time? What does it mean?

_____

_____

_____

2. Read John 20. Mary said to Peter and John, "They have taken the Lord out of the tomb, and we do not know where they have laid him" (v. 2). What had Mary heard Jesus say over and over? What does that say about being a disciple of Jesus?

_____

_____

_____

3. John reached the empty tomb before Peter but did not go in until Peter rushed in. Why would John hesitate?

_____

_____

_____

4. The tomb in which Jesus was laid was Joseph of Arimathea's tomb, a new and unused rich man's tomb. Describe what it was like.

_____

_____

_____

5. What did Peter and John see in the tomb? If the body of Jesus had been stolen, would it have looked like that?

_____

_____

_____

6. What is the incredible significance of the folded-up linen napkin or face cloth?

_____

_____

_____

7. In the midst of proclaiming the greatest miracle of all time, John noted that he outran Peter to the tomb three times. What does this tell us about all that we bring to the resurrection of Jesus? What's the good news in that?

_____

_____

_____

8. When John entered the empty tomb, it says that "he saw and believed" (John 20:8). The Greek word *pisteuō* is translated as "believe," but how can that be misleading in our present-day culture? What does *pisteuō* mean?

_____

_____

_____

9. Do you believe with that kind of belief? Explain your answer.

_____

_____

_____

10. Peter and John "believed," and "yet they did not understand the Scripture, that he must rise from the dead" (John 20:8–9). How can you fully believe while you still don't understand a lot of things in Scripture? What is the anchor that keeps you regardless of whatever else you understand or don't understand?

_____

_____

_____

11. When the two angels asked Mary why she was weeping, what could they have been thinking?

_____

_____

_____

12. Mary is so confused in her own sorrow that she doesn't even recognize Jesus. What's the warning here? How easy is it to miss the God of miracles?

_____

_____

_____

13. Jesus says the most beautiful word when He calls Mary by name. It came with the power of revelation. Have you heard Jesus call your name? It is my prayer that somehow you would know that He is calling you, that through the revelation of the Holy Spirit you would believe as they believed. Quiet your heart and soul and listen to that still, small voice inside. What is He saying to you?

_____

_____

_____

14. The disciples huddled together in fear behind locked doors. What happened to all the faith they once had? Why is fear so destructive?

_____

_____

_____

15. The disciples didn't expect Jesus to suddenly show up in the midst of their fear and doubt and speak peace to them. What barriers and barricades has He walked through in your life?

_____

_____

_____

16. What did Jesus mean when He said to the disciples, "Receive the Holy Spirit. If you forgive the sins of any, they are forgiven them; if you withhold forgiveness from any, it is withheld" (John 20:22–23)?

_____

_____

_____

17. By His resurrection, Jesus reconciled us to God, meaning that our relationship with God could return to what it was intended to be. How does the word *ruach* in Genesis 2:7 speak to the original creation and what our relationship to God was meant to be?

_____

_____

_____

18. Read Exodus 33:20–21. What was man's relationship with God like all throughout the Old Testament?

_____

_____

_____

19. In the upper room, when Jesus appears and breathes on the disciples, what was happening?

_____

_____

_____

20. So what in your life needs resurrecting? Maybe you need to walk up to the tomb, take a look inside, and be reminded that He's not in there. He's risen. Do you need Him to breathe on you?

_____

_____

_____

21. Jesus meets us not only in our sorrows and fears but also in our doubts. How does the resurrected Jesus reach out to Thomas, and how does Thomas respond to Jesus?

_____

_____

_____

_____

22. John ends his Gospel this way: "Now Jesus did many other signs in the presence of the disciples, which are not written in this book; but these are written so that you may believe [trust or _pisteuō_] that Jesus is the Christ, the Son of God, and that by believing you may have life in his name" (John 20:30–31). So let me ask you again: Do you need a miracle? Jesus is here, breathing new life. Will you bring all your unbelief, fall on your face, and believe in Him?

_____

_____

_____

_____

23. What miracle do you need? "You do not have, because you do not ask" (James 4:2). So name the need, write it out, lay it at the feet of Jesus, and trust Him. Is it an addiction? Cancer? Your marriage? A prodigal? What? Maybe you think your problem is too big for Him? He defeated death, hell, and the grave. He can handle whatever you bring Him. "Let us then with confidence draw near to the throne of grace, that we may receive mercy and find grace to help in time of need" (Heb. 4:16). So write out your need and cry out for a miracle.

_____

_____

_____

_____

24. Read Hebrews 11:6. The key is faith, and the good news is that if you think you don't have it, "faith comes from hearing, and hearing through the word of Christ" (Rom. 10:17). This means that if you don't have it, you can get it. It's simple. Listen. Believe. Do. Then pray with me the prayer that's at the end of this chapter and join me at the empty tomb.

_____

_____

_____

_____

CHAPTER 9

The Gift of the Holy Spirit—Do You Want to Know Christ and the Power of His Resurrection?

1. So how do we experience the unexplainable, the undeniable, the miraculous in our lives? Romans 4:17 is a good place to start. What does that tell us about God?

_____

_____

_____

_____

2. Read John 15. Describe what it means to "abide" in Christ.

_____

_____

_____

_____

3. Jesus says, "If the world hates you, know that it has hated me before it hated you" (John 15:18). Does the world hate you? If yes, in what ways have you experienced that hatred?

_____

_____

_____

4. Describe the worldview we are to have as believers. Check out John 15:12.

_____

_____

_____

5. What is the contrasting worldview of nonbelievers?

_____

_____

_____

6. What is the problem if we think we can get along in the world pretty good? Where is the constant drift of this culture going? What does Hebrews 6:19 tell us we must have if we are not going to drift in the wrong direction?

_____

_____

_____

7. Read John 15:20. What was the context in which Jesus previously said, "A servant is not greater than his master" (John 13:16)? How does this eliminate any notions of it being okay for believers to hate the world and be jerks?

_____

_____

_____

8. What does Jesus command us to do with every person as well as the way the world says we're to do everything? How is that exactly the opposite of what we often do?

_____

_____

_____

9. When it comes to loving the world system versus following Jesus' example and what He says, do you share the world's view of money? Do you give the first 10 percent of everything that comes in for the advancement of God's kingdom? Is that your bottom-line, basement-level beginning of generosity? What warning does Jesus give us in Matthew 6:21? How's your heart on this?

_____

_____

_____

10. The world says about sex and sexuality, "I do what I want with whom I want whenever I want, and I ask no one's permission." Is that your view as well? Describe your view.

_____

_____

_____

11. The world says about power and influence, "I am here to build my status and my own platform, to lift myself first above others, to get what's mine." Read Mark 10:45 and Philippians 2:5–11. Which model are you living? Can you really say you are living to serve others?

_____

_____

_____

12. How does Jesus' statement in John 15:23 contradict the popular belief that there's one God and many roads to Him or Her and you just pick your path? Does that trouble you?

_____

_____

_____

13. Jesus makes it clear that the world's hatred is going to be intense and rough, but in John 15:16, He offers a solution to the pain that we are going to experience because of our faith. What will help us to stand firm and remain rooted in the Word of God?

_____

_____

_____

14. Many churches tend to reduce the role of the Holy Spirit in the life of the believer to the giver of the gifts of the Spirit. The spiritual gifts are found in Romans 12, 1 Corinthians 12–14, and Ephesians 4, and understanding your spiritual gift(s) is very important. Write down the various gifts and which one or ones that you think are yours. Perhaps use our church assessment tool online as well, at https://coe22.com/gifts.

_____

_____

_____

_____

15. Ultimately, what is the only way to truly figure out your spiritual gift and what part of the body of Christ you should serve in for the advancement of God's kingdom? Are you using your gift now or taking practical steps to discover it?

_____

_____

_____

_____

16. Our focus here is not on spiritual gifts, but to what the primary evidence of the Holy Spirit is in the life of a believer. How is it stated in John 15:27? Read Acts 8:1–12. What was happening in Samaria through Philip that shows the primary evidence of the Holy Spirit?

_____

_____

_____

17. What is it that the Holy Spirit wants to do through your life? How is that reflected in the following Scriptures?

    John 14:12
    Acts 1:8
    Acts 2:1–8
    Luke 4:18–19
    Luke 1:38

_____

_____

_____

_____

18. After warning the disciples again that they would face great persecution, Jesus says, "It is to your advantage that I go away, for if I do not go away, the Helper will not come to you. But if I go, I will send him to you" (John 16:7). Based on John 14, 15, and 16, we're going to consider nine roles of the Holy Spirit in the life of the believer. Number one is that the Spirit of God empowers you to share your faith, which we just covered. Number two is that the Spirit of God is God's presence with you (John 14:16). What happens when you know God's presence is with you? See 1 John 4:18; 2 Timothy 1:7; and Joshua 1:6, 7, 9.

_____

_____

_____

19. According to John 14:26, what is the third role of the Holy Spirit in our lives?

_____

_____

_____

20. Number four is stated by Jesus: "And when he comes, he will convict the world concerning sin and righteousness and judgment" (John 16:8). Have you ever been convicted of sin? Describe what the Spirit showed you about yourself.

_____

_____

_____

21. What does it mean to be convicted of righteousness? Has the Holy Spirit ever shown you what your supposed righteousness looks like in the light of the perfect, righteous Son of God?

_____

_____

_____

22. The number five role of the Spirit is that of judgment. Apart from Jesus Christ, why should people be terrified? Are you prepared to stand before your Maker and give an account for your life?

_____

_____

_____

23. The apostle Paul says "that God's kindness is meant to lead you to repentance" (Romans 2:4). Do you understand what repentance is and that the Holy Spirit is wooing you into an eternal relationship with Jesus? How have you responded?

_____

_____

_____

24. The Spirit's number six role is "he will guide you into all the truth" (John 16:13). What does it mean that the Holy Spirit "guides" us in truth? How is there strength and control in that?

_____

_____

_____

25. The seventh thing that the Spirit of God does is lead us to worship Jesus (John 16:14). Read Genesis 24. How is this story a good picture of how the Holy Spirit purposefully works?

_____

_____

_____

26. How does one God in three persons—the Father, the Son, and the Holy Spirit—cooperate in our salvation?

_____

_____

_____

27. The number eight role is that the Holy Spirit helps us to pray to the Father in Jesus' name. What does Romans 8:26 add that He will do? What amazing promise is found in John 16:23–24? How do we often mess that up?

_____

_____

_____

28. The ninth thing the Holy Spirit does is to bring us peace (John 16:33). What tribulations are you facing? What is God's assurance and promise to us in these matters?

_____

_____

_____

_____

29. Are you in need of peace in some area of your life today? What is it? To you, Jesus says, "Come to me, all who labor and are heavy laden, and I will give you rest" (Matt. 11:28). "Rest" is "peace." Jesus is seated at the right hand of God interceding for us. What are you bringing to Him to find peace and rest?

_____

_____

_____

_____

30. I want you to join with me in the prayer at the end of this chapter. I want us to pray that the Spirit of God does exactly what Jesus promised, because we believe Jesus is who He says He is and He always keeps His promise. So come, Holy Spirit, come. Have Your way. Rule. Reign. Deliver. Save. Heal. Now go ahead and reach out to Jesus, and let's pray in belief and faith.

_____

_____

_____

_____

God is who He says He is, or He's not. I'm praying like crazy that you have chosen to believe, to *pisteuō*, in Him. I know it's hard, and you have an enemy who's working really hard to fill you with doubt and fear. But at the end of the day, do you want to doubt your doubts, or doubt your beliefs? I want to silence the doubts and believe my beliefs. Our King is seated on the throne at the right hand of God the Father. Jesus defeated death and the grave and paid the debt for our sin that we could not pay in ten thousand lifetimes. He did so because He loves us with an indescribable love, and He wants to return us to our Father. He holds the whole world, including you and me, in His hands. And not only that, but He has sent His very Spirit to help us. To fill us. Live in us. Empower us.

Our King is coming back. Maybe sooner rather than later. How will He find you when He does? Doubting? Believing? Between here and His return, He has commanded us to ask and to pray, so we will. We will do whatever He tells us to do. And that includes praying for the miraculous, the unexplainable, and the undeniable. Jesus is interceding for us at the right hand of God. He has the Father's ear. And you have His heart. He loves you more than you can fathom. There is no greater power and no greater love, so ask. Just ask.

When someone came to Jesus asking for a miracle in the Scriptures, three things were routinely needed: belief, hope, and faith. But, in most cases, they had very little. Like trace amounts. But Jesus never required that they muster some minimum threshold on the belief-o-meter. The apostle Paul says, "For it is God who works in you, both to will and to work for his good pleasure" (Phil. 2:13). If you let that sink in, it'll take the pressure off. God works in us. With that in mind, I'm praying that through the power of the Holy Spirit you will believe in, hope that, and have faith for. These three are the stuff that brings people like us pleading to the feet of Jesus.

It is entirely possible that the miracle you're praying for is waiting just on the other side of a small step of faith. Of obedience. Between now and then, I pray you and I live our lives believing in the risen Christ, doing what He tells us to do, and remembering that God raised Him to life, leaving an empty tomb.

The empty tomb changes everything about everything for everyone who would believe it. Why? Let me remind you of the words of Jesus, "All things are possible for one who believes" (Mark 9:23).

Would you join me one more time in the prayer at the end of this epilogue?

We Want to Hear from You

If you prayed to receive Christ while reading this book, or if you have questions about the faith, or if you need someone to pray with you, please contact me at my church, the Church of Eleven22. Folks at my church will pray with you if you email or call me at:

Joby.Martin@coe22.com

904-685-6722

I am not asking this of you so we can take some sort of weird satisfaction in adding you to a head count, but so we can encourage you and get you connected with a body, a local church. Christians are not meant to walk alone but in community. In fact, the enemy would really like for you to try and go it alone. So please, contact us and let us help you on your journey.

About the Authors

JOBY MARTIN is the founder and lead pastor of The Church of Eleven22 in Jacksonville, Florida. Since launching the church in 2012, he has led a movement for all people to discover and deepen a relationship with Jesus Christ. In addition to providing The Church of Eleven22 with vision and leadership, Pastor Joby is an author and a national and international preacher and teacher. He has been married to his wife, Gretchen, for over twenty years; they have a son, JP, and a daughter, Reagan.

CHARLES MARTIN is a *New York Times* bestselling author of seventeen novels, including his most recent, *The Record Keeper*. He has also authored two nonfiction books, *What If It's True?* and *They Turned the World Upside Down*. His work has been translated into more than thirty-six languages. He and his wife, Christy, have been married thirty years and have three sons. You can read more about him at https://charlesmartinbooks.com.